D0753425

BEAR HUNTING

By Tom Carpenter

Content Consultant
Bill Sherck
Outdoor Television Show Host

SportsZone

An Imprint of Abdo Publishing
abdopublishing.com

abdopublishing.com

Published by Abdo Publishing, a division of ABDO, PO Box 398166, Minneapolis, Minnesota 55439. Copyright © 2016 by Abdo Consulting Group, Inc. International copyrights reserved in all countries. No part of this book may be reproduced in any form without written permission from the publisher. SportsZone™ is a trademark and logo of Abdo Publishing.

Printed in the United States of America, North Mankato, Minnesota
042015
092015

Cover Photos: Lynn Bystrom/iStockphoto (foreground); Shutterstock Images (background)
Interior Images: Lynn Bystrom/iStockphoto, 1 (foreground); Shutterstock Images, 1 (background), 20; Dusty Photos/Blend Images/Corbis, 4–5; Alaska Stock Images/National Geographic Creative, 6; Nicolas McComber/iStockphoto, 9; Tory Kallman/Shutterstock Images, 10–11; iStockphoto, 12, 26; Jim David/ Shutterstock Images, 15; BG Smith/Shutterstock Images, 18–19; Sam Cook/ MCT/Newscom, 22; Jim Mone/AP Images, 24; Melissa Farlow/National Geographic Creative, 29; Lakeview Images/Shutterstock Images, 30–31; Neal Mishler/Alamy, 32; Justin Kral/Shutterstock Images, 34–35; Nate Allred/ Shutterstock Images, 36; Becky Bohrer/AP Images, 38; Nathan Allred/Alamy, 40; Earl Harper/Aurora Photos/Corbis, 42–43

Editor: Jon Westmark
Series Designer: Jake Nordby

Library of Congress Control Number: 2015901253

Cataloging-in-Publication Data
Carpenter, Tom.
 Bear hunting / Tom Carpenter.
   p. cm. -- (Hunting)
Includes bibliographical references and index.
ISBN 978-1-62403-831-0
1. Bear hunting--Juvenile literature.   I. Title.
799.2/78--dc23

                                                                2015901253

CONTENTS

Chapter 1

WELCOME TO BEAR HUNTING

It is late afternoon on an early autumn day. A young hunter walks through the leafy woods, rifle in hand. Some of the leaves are yellow, but few have dropped off the trees yet.

Camouflage helps hunters avoid being noticed by bears. States have different requirements for what hunters can wear.

The hunter arrives at a tree stand deep in the forest. Quietly he ties his unloaded rifle to a rope, climbs 15 feet (5 m) into the stand, and attaches his safety harness. He pulls the rifle

Black bears prefer to have a lot of land to roam without other bears.

up with the rope and loads the firearm. Then he sits down for a long and quiet wait.

A bait pile sits 20 yards (18 m) from the base of the tree. The pile has a variety of foods that bears love. Its purpose is to attract a bear from its hiding place deep in the brush. In a forested area this vast and thick, this is one of the only ways to shoot a bear.

As the sun goes slowly down, squirrels look for food in the woods. Songbirds chirp on nearby branches. But when the sun dips below the trees, the woods become silent.

The hunter sits up and becomes more alert. Dusk is coming. At this time of year, hungry bears often move in the evening, toward the end of legal hunting hours.

A twig snaps. The hunter's heart beats faster. A dark form drifts along the game trail, approaching cautiously: It's a black bear!

The bear nears the clearing where the hunter left the bait. It is a big bear. The young hunter wonders if the bear will hear his heart pounding. There is still enough light to make a good shot. Quietly he brings his rifle up. He takes aim and slowly squeezes the trigger.

With the sound of the shot, the bear jumps in the air and then runs into the brush. But through the branches the hunter sees the large animal fall. The hunter sits down, knees shaking. He just got a bear!

Bear Hunting History

In North America, bears have been hunted since before European settlers arrived. Native Americans hunted bears for food. They used bear hides in ceremonies and as blankets in winter.

When settlers cleared forests across the continent, bears were forced into smaller areas of wilderness. The settlers also hunted the bears. There were no rules about how many bears the hunters could take. The bear population fell.

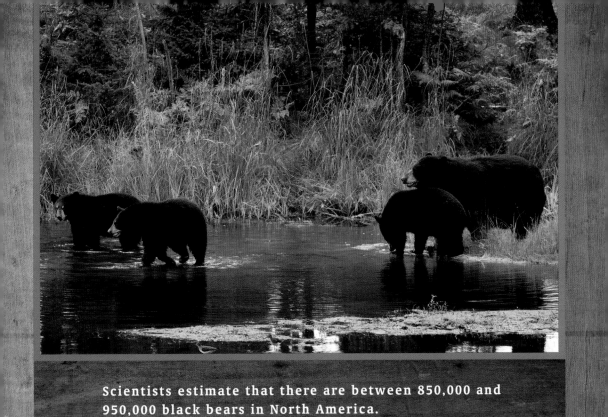

Scientists estimate that there are between 850,000 and 950,000 black bears in North America.

But now bears are expanding their range again. In many places, bears live near humans. With healthy populations of black bears and brown bears in the United States and Canada, hunters can harvest bears. Today people hunt bears for the meat and hide. They also do it because bear hunting is an exciting challenge.

Chapter 2

BIOLOGY AND HABITAT

In North America, people hunt both black bears and brown bears. To successfully hunt bears, it is important to understand their physical traits, habitats, and habits.

Despite their size, bears are good at climbing trees.

Black Bears

Most black bears are just that—black. Some may feature spots or V-shaped patches of white fur on their chests. Male black bears, known as boars, weigh anywhere from 200 to 400 or

Black bears do not eat while they are in hibernation.

more pounds (91–181 kg) when fully grown. Females, called sows, weigh 100 to 300 pounds (45–136 kg). Black bears have small ears and eyes, a stubby tail, and one-to two-inch-long claws. Black bears use their claws to climb trees.

Black bears live in large areas of continuous woodlands. Swamps, marshes, forested mountains, and foothills are also good bear habitats. Bears are adapting to the environment humans have created, and some bears are found in areas where big, thick woods mix with farmland.

Black bears are omnivores. That means they eat both plant material and meat. Bears eat berries, fruits, nuts, acorns, grasses, shoots, mushrooms, and farm crops such as corn and oats. Bears will also hunt small animals and look for carrion. Black bears feed most actively at dawn and

Some Black Bears Are Not Black

Not every black bear is black! Some black bears are brown. Others have cinnamon-colored coats. There are even some blond black bears. They are the same species, just different colors! These different-colored bears are most common in the US Pacific Northwest and western Canada but may be found anywhere across black bear range.

dusk. But when food is scarce, they will look for food at any time of day.

Black bears breed in early summer. The sow gives birth to one to five cubs during hibernation in winter. All bears hibernate. Before hibernation they spend the autumn eating as much as they can to build up fat for a long winter of little activity.

Brown Bears

Brown bears are larger than black bears. Adult boars weigh from 500 to 1,000 pounds (227–454 kg) or more. Sows weigh from 500 to 700 pounds (227–318 kg). Named for their rich brown coat, brown bears have long claws to help catch prey. Brown bears are fast. They can run up to 30 miles per hour (48 km/h) for short bursts.

Brown bears live around coasts, foothills, mountains, and cold and treeless areas called tundra. Ideal brown bear habitats offer a mix of forest or brushland and open areas or meadows.

Brown bears can be distinguished by a distinctive shoulder hump. These are muscles that help the bear dig.

Brown bears are also omnivores. They eat almost anything they can find or hunt. In springtime brown bears eat grasses, shoots, insects, and carrion. In summer they like to eat berries. Brown bears also hunt young deer or caribou and dig up ground squirrels and gophers to eat. In late summer and fall, many brown bears eat salmon from

Grizzly Bears

Grizzly bears and brown bears are the same species. Brown bears are larger and live on the ocean coast. Grizzly bears live in the inland mountains and tundra. Grizzly bears are generally smaller than brown bears by 200 to 300 pounds (91–136 kg).

rivers and streams. Brown bears feed whenever they are hungry, which is often.

Brown bears breed from late spring to midsummer. The sow gives birth to cubs, usually two but up to four, in her winter den. She protects the cubs for two years as they grow up. Brown bears feed heavily in autumn to put on fat for winter. Bears hibernate during the long winter, emerging hungry from their dens in spring.

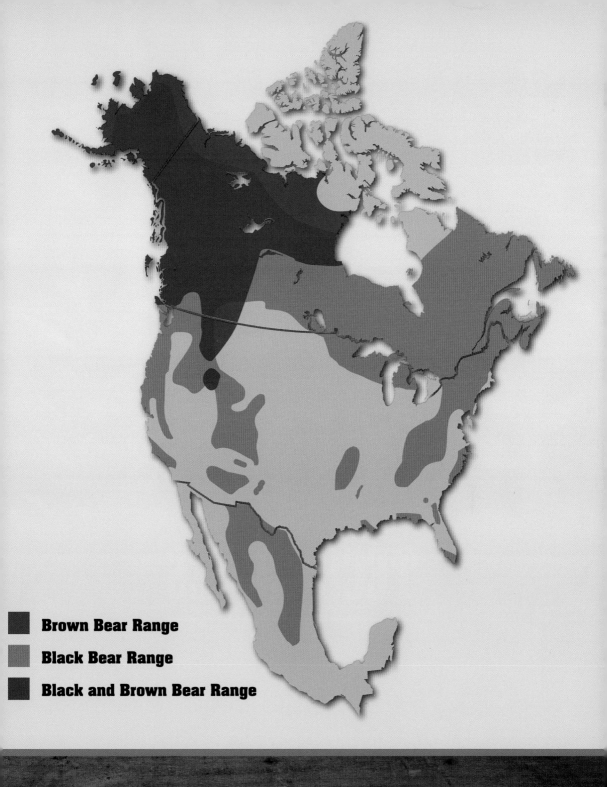

Brown Bear Range

Black Bear Range

Black and Brown Bear Range

Bear territory has rebounded in recent years. But most brown bears still live in Canada and Alaska. Laws protect them in the rest of the United States.

Chapter 3

TECHNIQUES

Wildlife managers allow bear hunting seasons when bear populations are high. Because bears are so elusive and bear habitats are so big, there is little danger of damaging the

Black bears prefer dense forests where there is plenty of vegetation to eat.

population. The goal of bear hunting is to thin the population so the remaining bears have plenty to eat and enough territory to roam.

Bears are difficult to hunt. They have great senses. Hunters need to understand bear

Bears have color vision, which helps them identify
berries and fruits to eat.

senses to get a bear in their sights. They also need to use special techniques to go undetected.

Bear Senses

Bears have an excellent sense of smell. A bear's nose is 10 times more sensitive than a bloodhound's. This helps bears find food, whether they are looking for berries or digging for gophers. But this awesome sense of smell also helps bears identify danger. Hunters must stay downwind from the bear to avoid detection.

With their small ears, bears do not hear every sound in the woods. But they identify sounds that are out of place. So hunters must be quiet. It helps to wear soft clothes, such as fleece, that do not make much noise while moving.

Bears have only average eyesight. Their great sense of smell and good ears make up for this. Bears know their habitat. They will sense that something is out of place if hunters move around too much.

Hunting bait must have a strong smell so that bears can find it from a long distance.

Hunting Over Bait

Black bears often live where the cover is thick and widespread. They are scattered across large areas. This makes it almost impossible to see a bear by waiting along a trail or walking through the forest.

This is why hunters use bait to lure bears to certain spots. The hunter sits in a tree stand near the bait and waits for the bear to appear. Apples, old bread, donuts, pastries, and other baked goods are great bait. Adding grease helps too. It smells great to bears. Oats, corn, or other grains soaked in molasses also work.

Hunters often set up tree stands weeks before the season opens. They also make bait stations. They dig a small hole in the ground and place the bait in it. Some put logs over the bait to make the bears work to get to the food. This also keeps small animals out. It is important to check the bait every couple days and add bait when bears start showing up and eating.

Game Camera Essentials

Placing a game camera at a bait site helps hunters see the bears that are eating the bait. It also shows what time the bears are most active. Most hunters check cameras and replenish bait only at midday, when bears are least likely to be in the area.

Setting up a tree stand well before hunting helps ensure that the hunter's scent does not scare away any bears.

Bear hunters often place a couple of tree stands around the bait so the site can be hunted under different wind conditions. The wind should blow from the bait to the hunter so that the bear will not smell him. Good trees for a stand offer some leaves as cover. Hunters should also cut shooting lanes for a clear shot from the stand to the bait site. Good distances are about 20 yards (18 m) away for bowhunting and 20 to 30 yards (18–27 m) away for rifle hunting.

Bears may come to the bait site at dawn. But hunters cannot get into their stands that early without scaring the bear off. Hunting in the afternoon and evening, until legal shooting hours end, is most productive.

The best time to take a shot is when the bear is sideways, or broadside. Baiting gives hunters an opportunity to look the bear over and perhaps identify it as a boar they want to shoot. While it is legal to shoot sows, some hunters prefer shooting boars. Sows may have cubs they need to take care of.

Spot-and-Stalk Hunting

Hunters do not usually bait brown bears. Hunters spot-and-stalk these bears because they live in open areas. In mountains, black bears can be spotted and stalked too.

To spot-and-stalk, hunters move into the wind through bear territory. They keep to high ground so they can see

Comfortable shoes and quiet clothing are important
for spot-and-stalk hunting.

well. They walk below ridgetops so they do not "skyline" or silhouette against the sky. It is important to stop often to look for bears around the surrounding countryside with binoculars or a spotting scope.

When hunters see a bear, they identify the bear's line of travel, taking note of landmarks. They use geography and terrain features to stay out of sight. They also keep the wind blowing from the bear to themselves.

When in range of the bear, hunters take their first clear shot. Most spot-and-stalk hunters use rifles. They get within 100 to 200 yards (91–183 m) of the bear and rest the rifle on a fixed object to keep their aim steady.

Other Bear Hunting Techniques

There are several other ways to hunt bears. People use different techniques depending on the terrain.

One method is float hunting. Hunters get in boats or canoes and float along a body of water. They look for bears feeding near shore. When they spot a bear, they park the watercraft, get out, and stalk on foot.

In places with thick cover, sometimes large groups of hunters get together and walk. They try to get bears to move toward other hunters who are waiting ahead. This is called a drive.

In meadows or open areas, hunters sometimes attract bears by using calls that imitate injured animals. Bears that hear the calls may come running in search of an easy meal.

Hunting with Dogs

In some places it is legal to hunt black bears with dogs. Scent-driven coonhounds, such as black-and-tans, treeing walkers, blueticks, redbones, and Plotts, are great dogs for bear hunting. The barking dogs chase a bear until the bear climbs a tree to escape. Then the hunters approach to shoot the bear. But many hunters call off the dogs and let the bear live. An exciting chase can be rewarding enough!

It usually takes a pack of dogs to chase a black bear into a tree. The bear may not retreat from a single dog.

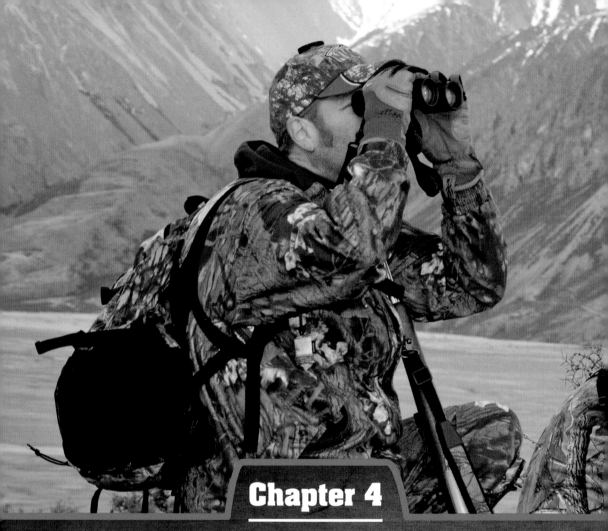

Chapter 4

EQUIPMENT AND SKILLS

Most of the gear used for hunting other big game will also work for bear hunting. But successful bear hunting does require some special skills and equipment.

Staying low and using binoculars help hunters see bears before being seen.

Bear Hunting Equipment

Bears are tough, muscular animals that can be hard to kill. Large-caliber rifles are best for bringing a bear down. Semiautomatic rifles can shoot many cartridges in a short period of time.

Quick movements can startle bears, so it is best to take aim slowly.

It may seem like this would be best for hunting bears. But bolt-action rifles also have benefits. They provide excellent accuracy and reliable cartridge cycling for follow-up shots.

For close-range hunting or for hunting down a wounded bear, some hunters prefer a shotgun instead of a rifle. They load the shotgun with slugs. Slugs are heavier than rifle bullets and deliver more power.

Some people hunt bears with bows and arrows. Bows for bear hunting need to be accurate from 20 to 30 yards (18–27 m). Their tips, or broadheads, should be razor sharp. Hunting bears with a bow is challenging because precise shot placement is very important.

Regardless of what kind of weapons hunters use, they need a reliable tree stand to hunt over bait. This allows them to get up off the forest floor and above the bear's line of sight. This may also keep their scent above the bear. Hunters should not use homemade tree stands. These are often unreliable and can fall down.

MAKING THE SHOT

Camouflage: Camouflage helps the hunter go unnoticed.

Bolt Action: Bolt-action rifles allow the hunter to efficiently cycle through cartridges.

Prone Shot: Lying down helps the hunter stay out of view and steady the shot.

Scope: A high-powered scope helps the hunter place the shot.

Support: A gun support adds additional control for long-range shots.

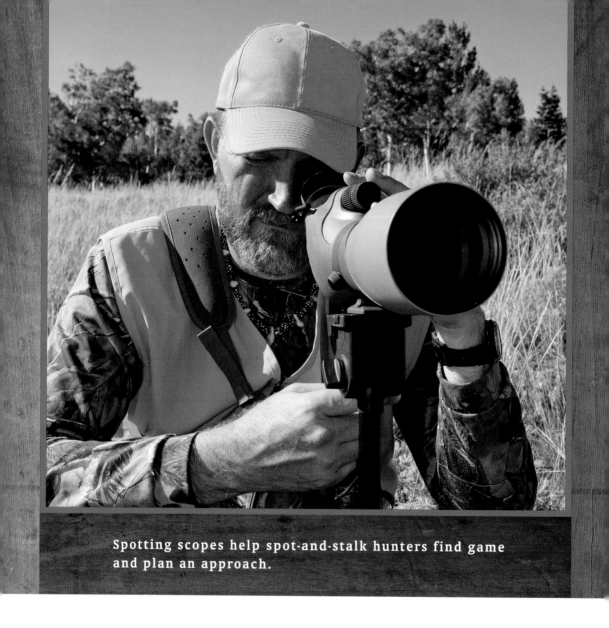

Spotting scopes help spot-and-stalk hunters find game and plan an approach.

When stalking bears in open terrain, good optics are

a must. A pair of 8- to 10-power binoculars is good for

spotting bears. A 20-power spotting scope is good for a

close-up view. Binoculars are also important in the woods

for evaluating bears at bait piles. Good optics can reveal if a bear is a boar or a sow.

Bear Hunting Skills

The hunting techniques leading up to the shot are important, but successful bear hunters must also be prepared to finish the hunt. They should be able to shoot confidently with accuracy and precision and know how to track wounded bears.

Whether hunting with a rifle, shotgun, or bow, hunters should practice shooting at targets before the season. Sighting-in is a top priority for most hunters. It allows the hunter to adjust the scope or sights and make sure the gun shoots accurately. Bears will be about 20 to 30 yards (18–27 m) away if the hunter is baiting and 100 to 200 yards (91–183 m) out if the hunter is stalking. So it is good to sight-in at these distances.

For hunters who get a shot at a bear, it is important to place the shot in the right spot. A poor shot may result in

A black bear quartering away at a gradual angle is best. If the bear is walking away at too steep of an angle, the hunter may not have a shot.

a long tracking job. Bears are very tough and can be hard to find.

The best shot is when the bear is broadside. The hunter should aim just behind the front leg, halfway between the bear's back and chest. Another good shot is when the bear is quartering away. This is when the bear is walking away from the hunter at an angle. The hunter should aim for the middle of the bear's chest. This will take out both lungs.

Even with good shots, bears do not always drop right away. Sometimes a hunter has to trail the animal.

It is a good idea to wait a half hour after the shot before trailing a bear. This gives the animal a chance to find a place to lie down. If the hunter follows the animal too soon, it may not stop running. If this happens, fat may seal up the wound, making it so there is no blood to follow on the ground.

Most hunters track bears with a partner. That way one hunter can concentrate on the ground and follow the blood trail. The other hunter can stay alert, ready to shoot if the bear appears.

It is not a good idea to track bears alone. Black bears do not attack often, but they are capable of it. Brown bears and grizzlies are more likely to attack.

A tracking partner can also help transport the bear out of the woods after it is killed.

All bears must be tagged once they are killed. Hunters get a limited number of tags. Tagging the animal ensures that people do not use their tags more than once. After tagging the bear, hunters must field dress the animal. The hunter removes the internal organs of the bear. This helps the meat cool quickly and prevents it from going bad. It is illegal to waste meat from a harvested animal. Many hunters prepare and cook the meat for themselves. Some donate it to organizations for others to enjoy.

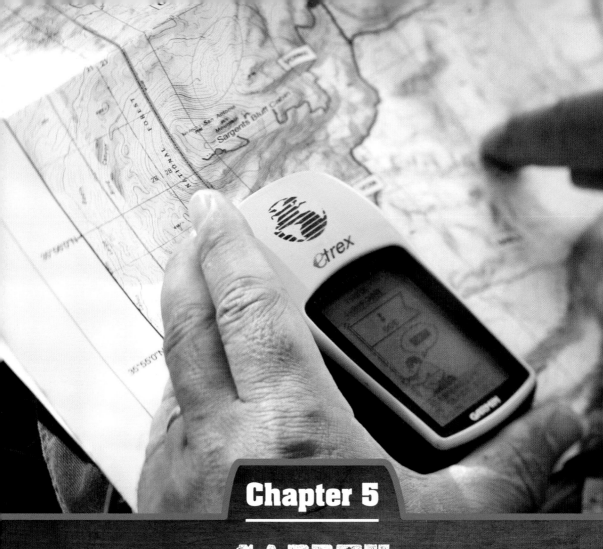

Chapter 5

SAFETY

Bears are usually hunted in big, wild country.
It can be easy to get lost. It is important for
hunters to let someone know where they will be
hunting and when they expect to return. Hunters

Hunters can plan their route using GPS to help prevent getting lost.

can carry a GPS unit to monitor their movement. A compass can serve as a backup navigational tool.

Falling out of a tree stand is another potential danger while bear hunting. Hunters use safety straps when they put up stands and climb into them. This helps prevent falls. It is important to use only approved tree stands and to put them up according to the manufacturer's instructions.

Once hunters are in their tree stands, they pull up their unloaded firearms, or bows and arrows, using rope. This is one of many precautions hunters take with their firearms. Most states require all hunters to take a firearms or hunter's safety course before hunting.

TAB-K Formula

One good way to remember how to be safe with a firearm is by following the TAB-K formula:

T—Treat every firearm as if it were loaded at all times.

A—Always point the gun in a safe direction.

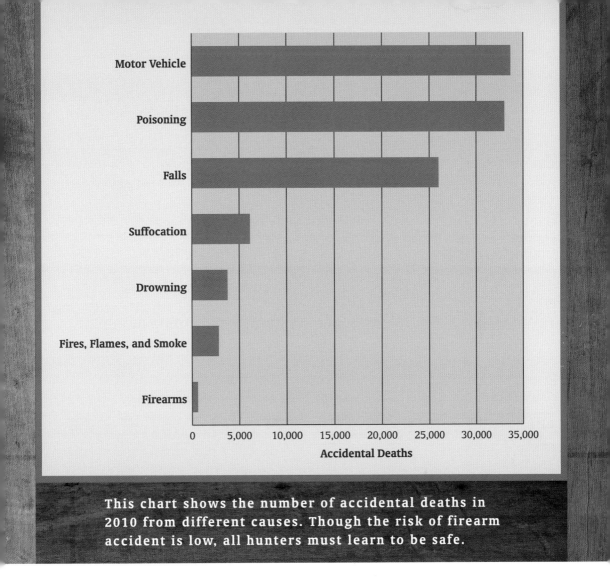

This chart shows the number of accidental deaths in 2010 from different causes. Though the risk of firearm accident is low, all hunters must learn to be safe.

B—Be certain of your target and what's beyond it.

K—Keep your finger outside of the trigger guard until you are ready to shoot.

GLOSSARY

bolt-action rifle
A firearm with a hand-operated action that is pulled up and back to eject a cartridge and pushed forward and down to load a new one.

broadside
The position a bear is in when it stands with one side exposed to the hunter. This is one of the best shots to take on a bear.

caliber
The side-to-side measurement of the cartridge.

carrion
The meat and remains left over from a dead animal.

cartridge
A combination of primer, brass casing, powder, and bullet that is loaded into a rifle and fired.

game camera
A digital, motion-sensitive camera set up to capture images of game moving through an area. Hunters use game cameras as scouting tools.

shooting lane
An opening cut through branches and brush to make sure a hunter in a blind or tree stand has a clear shot at a target.

shotgun
A type of firearm loaded with a shotgun shell consisting of primer, plastic casing, and a wad holding small metal balls or a slug.

slug
A single projectile or bullet loaded into a shotgun shell and fired through a shotgun's barrel.

spotting scope
A high-power optical device used to study game at long distances. Some spotting scopes zoom through a range of powers.

FOR MORE INFORMATION

Further Reading

Llanas, Sheila Griffin. *Grizzly Bears*. Minneapolis: Abdo Publishing, 2013.

McDowell, Pamela. *Black Bears*. New York: AV2 by Weigl, 2013.

McNeice, Connie-Lee. *Big Game*. New York: AV2 by Weigl, 2013.

Websites

To learn more about Hunting, visit **booklinks.abdopublishing.com.** These links are routinely monitored and updated to provide the most current information available.

INDEX

ABOUT THE AUTHOR

Tom Carpenter is a father, a sportsman, and an outdoor writer. He has introduced many children, including his three sons, to the thrills and rewards of hunting. A native son of Wisconsin who always has part of his heart in South Dakota, he planted roots in the middle. He lives with his family near the shores of Bass Lake, Minnesota.